Building a Tree House

Select a tree, draw your design, then watch as the tree house is built before your eyes.

by **Sam Patras**

800-445-5985
www.etacuisenaire.com

Building a Tree House
ISBN 0-7406-4150-6
ETA 383111

ETA/Cuisenaire • Vernon Hills, IL 60061-1862
800-445-5985 • www.etacuisenaire.com

Series © 2006 by ETA/Cuisenaire®

Original version published by Nelson Australia Pty Limited (2002).
This edition is published by arrangement with Thomson Learning
Australia.

ETA/Cuisenaire
Manager of Product Development: Mary Watanabe
Creative Services Manager: Barry Daniel Petersen
Production Manager: Jeanette Pletsch
Lead Editor: Betty Hey
Copy Editor: Barbara Wrobel
Production Artist: Diana Chiropolos
Graphic Designer: Amy Endlich

Photographs and cover by Fotograffiti
Illustrations on pp. 6–7 by Guy Holt

Teacher consultant: Garry Chapman, Ivanhoe Grammar School

Printed in China.

06 07 08 09 10 11 12 13 14 15   10 9 8 7 6 5 4 3 2 1

CONTENTS

Chapter One

Choose a Tree

If you want to build a tree house, you'll need an adult to help you. But there are some things you can do yourself.

Before you start, the first and most important thing to do is to find the right tree.

Look at each tree in your yard.
- Is the height right?
- Is it healthy?
- Is the tree fully grown? If the tree isn't fully grown, then your tree house might shift, fall down, or become **unstable**.

too high

no branches

not strong enough

perfect

Chapter Two

Create Your Design

The next thing you can do is come up with
a design. Consider the following things—

• How high off the ground do you want the
  tree house to be?

• How will you get up there?

• How big will your tree house be?

Now, draw a sketch of your tree house to see how it might look. You may need to draw a few sketches before you come up with the one that suits your tree.

MY TREE HOUSE

Once you've chosen a design, you'll
need to draw a **formal** plan that includes
measurements. You will need to get an adult
to help you with this.

Then you will need a list of materials
to build your tree house.

Here is a list of materials Mr. Lee will need to get at the hardware store.

- Nail plates—flat steel plates
- Carriage bolts, nuts, washers
- Large screws and washers
- Hinges—for doors
- Surface bolts—for doors
- Door latch—for doors
- Screws and nails
- Ridge flashing—to be used where the roof joins at the peak to keep out rain
- Roof join, 1 strip
- Paintable waterproof sealant, 2 tubes—to seal up gaps and keep out the weather
- Premix concrete—just add water for instant concrete!

Chapter Three

Get ready

Next stop is the **lumber** yard to buy the timber. Mr. Lee checks the **plywood** to make sure it is nice and flat. Plywood is used on the walls and roof of the tree house.

Here is a list of materials Mr. Lee needs to buy from the lumber yard.

- Posts—for the base of the tree house
- Joists—a full length of timber or steel for support
- Bearers—pieces of wood that sit on the tree house stumps
- Stair runners—rods or grooves on which something slides
- Stair rail and posts
- Stair landing safety boards
- Plywood
- Framing for tree house

Mr. Lee is looking for good straight pieces of timber to work with.

Mr. Lee will use many different tools while he is building the tree house. See if you can name them all.

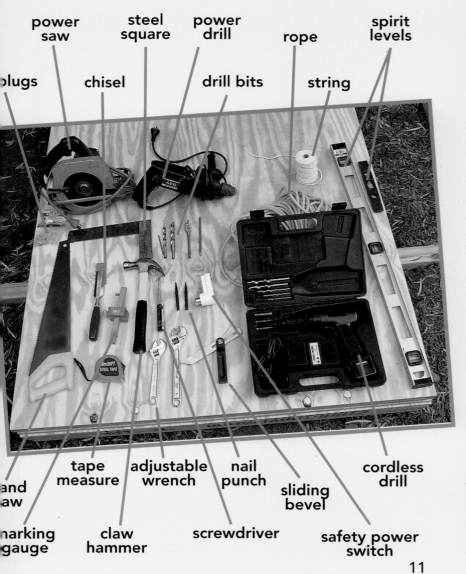

power saw   steel square   power drill   rope   spirit levels

plugs   chisel   drill bits   string

hand saw

marking gauge   tape measure   claw hammer   adjustable wrench   nail punch   screwdriver   sliding bevel   cordless drill   safety power switch

Before building begins, Mr. Lee lays out all his materials to check that he has everything he needs.

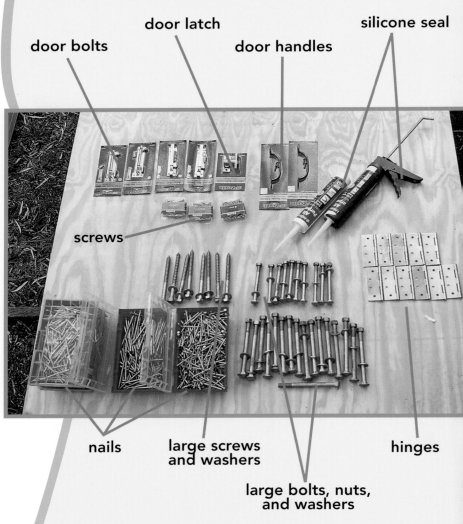

door bolts

door latch

door handles

silicone seal

screws

nails

large screws and washers

large bolts, nuts, and washers

hinges

Chapter Four

Start Building

Now we are ready to start building. Mr. Lee digs the **foundation** holes. He uses a tape measure to make sure he digs the holes in the right places.

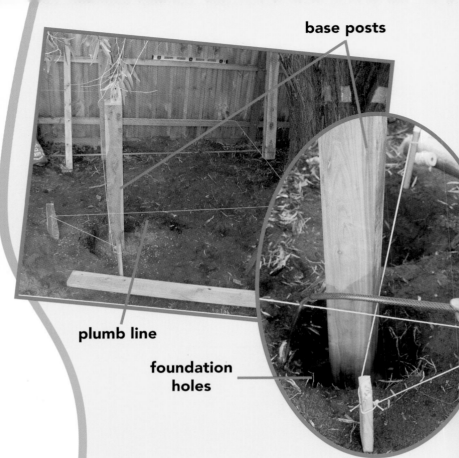

base posts

plumb line

foundation holes

After the foundation holes are dug, Mr. Lee lays out the plumb line. A plumb line is a line of string used to make sure that the base posts will be straight.

Now we can clearly see the area that the tree house will cover. Mr. Lee then puts the base posts in the foundation holes.

All the base posts must be the correct height and level. If not, you'll end up with a very wobbly, crooked tree house! You can check this by using a spirit level.

A spirit level is an instrument used to find out whether a surface is straight, both horizontally (across) and vertically (up and down).

The spirit level is straight when the bubble is exactly between the lines.

The cement around this post has set hard so the post cannot move.

Mr. Lee fills in the holes with premix cement and pours in water. Mr. Lee leaves the cement to set overnight.

Next, Mr. Lee cuts the base posts and cross beams. He cuts them all at the same time to make sure they fit neatly. He also drills the holes for the carriage bolts, so it is easier to hammer the bolts into the timber.

base post

carriage bolt

cross beam

Mr. Lee uses a safety power switch when using the power saw to cut timber. In the case of an emergency, the safety power switch will switch off. This will protect Mr. Lee from being **electrocuted** [ee-LEK-tro-kew-ted].

Now it's time to build the steps that will make it easier to get to your tree house.

The first part of the steps is the frame. Once the frame has been set up, Mr. Lee will build each individual step. While he is building the steps, the post holes can be filled in.

The steps are nailed into the frame.

You don't have to be an adult to fill in a hole!

Next, the floor is nailed on. Now it's starting to look like a tree house!

Mr. Lee uses a nail punch to push down any nails sitting up above the floor surface. This makes it safe to walk on without shoes.

hammer

nail punch

Mr. Lee uses earplugs when he's building so his ears are not damaged by loud noise.

Once the floor is finished, it is time to add some walls. It is easier for Mr. Lee to build the walls at ground level.

When the walls are made, they are carried up to the tree house and nailed in place.

Ask an adult before you use the hammer or nails. Practice hammering nails using scraps of wood.

windows

Don't forget to give your tree house some windows. The windows on this tree house are long and narrow so that they are safe. No one could ever fall through these windows.

Now we've got windows, but it's feeling a bit too breezy. It might be time to add a roof.

Chapter Five

Have Fun!

roof

double doors

After the roof goes on, we need a door. This design is for double doors that open on to the **balcony**. Finally, Mr. Lee will add a railing around the balcony and down the steps.

The posts on the railing should be close together so that even very small children will be safe from falling through.

Now we can all play safely in the tree house!

That's it. The tree house is built. Now you can start having fun.

Glossary

balcony an upstairs deck with a railing

electrocuted [ee-LEK-tro-kew-ted] injured or killed by electricity

formal following accepted rules or regulations

foundation the lowest part of a building

lumber partly cut and prepared timber

plywood a board made of thin layers of wood stuck together

unstable likely to change or collapse

Index